CP2.0 Mentor Text
2016
Property of Gr2
CPCSC

DESERT GIANT

TREE
TALES

DESERT GIANT

The World of the Saguaro Cactus

BARBARA BASH

Sierra Club Books for Children • San Francisco

To Audrey Benedict, who first led me out into the desert, and the Tohono O'odham Indians (the Desert People), who live in the saguaro world

The Sierra Club, founded in 1892 by John Muir, has devoted itself to the study and protection of the earth's scenic and ecological resources — mountains, wetlands, woodlands, wild shores and rivers, deserts and plains. The publishing program of the Sierra Club offers books to the public as a nonprofit educational service in the hope that they may enlarge the public's understanding of the Club's basic concerns. The point of view expressed in each book, however, does not necessarily represent that of the Club. The Sierra Club has some sixty chapters in the United States and Canada. For information about how you may participate in its programs to preserve wilderness and the quality of life, please address inquiries to Sierra Club, 85 Second Street, San Francisco, CA 94105, or visit our website at www.sierraclub.org.

All calligraphy by Barbara Bash

Library of Congress Cataloging-in-Publication Data

Bash, Barbara.
    Desert giant: the world of the saguaro cactus/by Barbara Bash.
  — 1st ed.
     p. cm.
    Summary: Documents the life cycle and ecosystem of the giant
    saguaro cactus and the desert animals it helps to support.
    ISBN: 1-57805-085-5 (pb)
  1. Saguaro – Juvenile literature. 2. Saguaro – Ecology – Juvenile
literature. 3. Desert ecology – Juvenile literature. 4. Botany –
Ecology – Juvenile literature. [1. Saguaro. 2. Cactus.
3. Desert ecology. 4. Ecology.] 1. Title.
QK495.C11B32 1989
583'.47 – dc19   88-4706

Printed in China

25 24 23 22 21 20

A strange and wonderful tree grows in the desert. It is called a saguaro (sa-WAHR-o) cactus, and its Latin name is *Cereus giganteus*.

There are many unusual shapes in the saguaro world. Walking out among them, you might feel as though you're surrounded by people – the Saguaro People.

The saguaro grows in the Sonoran desert, which stretches through parts of Arizona, California, and Mexico. This cactus can grow as tall as fifty feet, weigh up to several tons, and live for two hundred years.

The saguaro's sharp spines protect it from harm. The accordion-like pleats in its skin expand in the rain, storing extra water for the long dry times.

When you stand in the desert, everything is quiet. But if you listen closely, you can hear the sound of the wind moving past the spines. HISSSSSSSSSS...

Now there is another sound: tap...
tap-tap...The holes you see in the
saguaro trunk are made by the
"carpenter bird"—the Gila (HEE-la)
woodpecker. In the spring, the male
pecks deeply into the soft flesh of
the cactus to make a room for
his mate's eggs to hatch.

The saguaro flesh forms
a hard, callous lining
around the nests. When
the cactus dies and
decomposes, these
hollow forms are left
behind on the ground.
They are called "saguaro
boots" by the Indians,
who use them as food
containers.

Male

Saguaro boot

Female

When the Gila woodpecker moves out of its nest, the elf owl moves in. This is the tiniest owl in the world, measuring just five inches long. The elf owl is nocturnal, hunting for small insects, centipedes, and scorpions at night and sleeping in the nest during the day. Because of the thick lining and the moisture stored in the saguaro's flesh, the nest stays cool even on the hottest days.

Harris' hawks are the largest birds to make their homes in the saguaro. They raise their young in nests of twigs lined with leaves and grasses. Living in cooperative societies, much like wolves, up to four hawks can inhabit the same territory.

Sometimes the hawks use each other as perches. As many as three birds have been seen stacked on top of a saguaro! This is called Back Standing.

Back Standing

Nighttime. The moon shines in the dark sky. It is May, time for the saguaro to blossom. Out of the top of the cactus, high above the ground, the buds emerge and open into large, milky-white flowers with yellow centers. Each flower opens only once, in the cool of the night, and closes by the following afternoon.

Suddenly you hear a flapping of wings. A long-nosed bat has come to drink the nectar hidden deep in the center of the flower. As the bat drinks, the pollen dust sticks to its face and is carried along to pollinate the next bloom.

The next morning the white-winged doves arrive. They like to drink the flower nectar, too. One lands on top of the saguaro and dunks its head way inside. A queen butterfly alights on a petal, and a bee circles around, buzzing. Every creature that drinks the nectar picks up more pollen and carries it on to fertilize the next flower. When the flower is fertilized, the fruit can begin to form.

Stamen—
the male part
of the flower
that produces
the pollen

Stigma—
the female part
that catches
the pollen

Ovary—
the container
for the eggs
(the fruit will
form here)

Style—
the slender tube
that carries
the pollen
to the eggs

It is very hot out under the desert sun. By early afternoon, the flowers that opened the night before have closed, and the doves have flown into the shade to rest.

y June, the saguaro blossoms have
ried into brown stalks, and fruit
as formed from the bases. The
eeds are ripening, and the fruit
egins to split open, revealing its
right red insides.

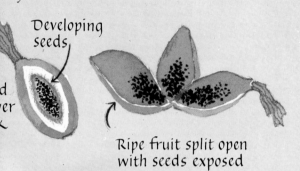

Developing
seeds

Ripe fruit split open
with seeds exposed

s they have been doing for
enturies, the Tohono O'odham
toh-HO-no o-O-dahm) Indians
egin the saguaro-fruit harvest.
he young women and children
o out into the desert with
uckets and gathering poles
nade of saguaro ribs bound
ogether. Wooden crosspieces are
vired onto the top and middle,
orming the prongs that pull
he ripe fruit down.

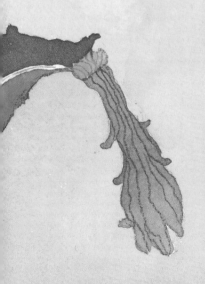

The children try to catch the
fruit as it falls. Sometimes they
steal a taste of the sweet, juicy pulp.

As the fruit is knocked down, the
women scoop the bright red pulp
full of tiny black seeds into buckets.
When the buckets are full and heavy,
they are carried back to the camp.

The women leave the red outer hulls
behind on the ground, open and
facing up to the sky. This is the
O'odham offering for rain.

At the campsite, the men gather wood for the fire, and the old women remove any pebbles from the fruit pulp. Then the pulp is mixed with water and cooked for a long time until it is thick and sweet. Finally, the cooked pulp is poured through wire mesh to separate the juice from the seeds.

The O'odham make jams and candies, syrups and wines out of the saguaro fruit. Harvest is a time of celebration because there is good saguaro food to eat and soon the rains will come.

Back at the saguaro, more fruit
is ripening. The curved-billed
thrasher comes to eat the
sweet pulp, and harvester ants
scurry around gathering the seeds.
The horned lizard waits by the
fallen fruit for the ants to walk by.
In a flash he catches one with his
long, fast, sticky tongue.

Nighttime. More fruit has dropped to the ground, and the air is cool. A coyote arrives to lick the fruit pulp out of the fallen rinds. Nearby, some javelina (hav-a-LEEN-a) pigs grunt and snort as they scoop up the sweet fruit.

It is a feasting time for the Indians, animals, birds, and ants. Everyone loves the saguaro fruit.

After providing food and homes
for so many creatures, the saguaro
eventually dies. Sometimes old age
and weakening tissue make it prey
to bacteria. The soft outer flesh falls
away, exposing the saguaro ribs,
which spread out like a big whisk
broom. At other times, strong winds
or lightning knock the saguaro
to the ground, where it gradually
decomposes.

Now a whole new set of creatures
moves in to live in the saguaro. . . .

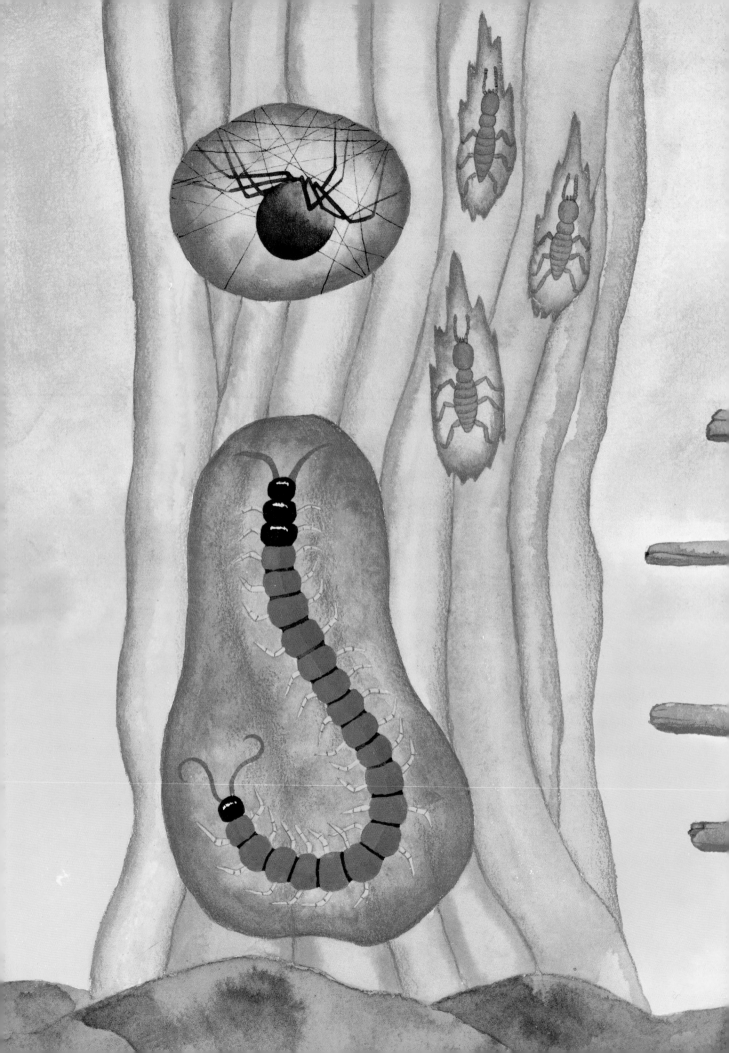

side the dead saguaro, termites
hew the wood. A black widow
pider spins her web. The giant
esert centipede searches for insects.
n top of a downed saguaro,

a banded gecko basks in the sun,
while underneath, a cactus mouse
stores seeds in its cheek pouches
and a spotted night snake curls
in the cool darkness.

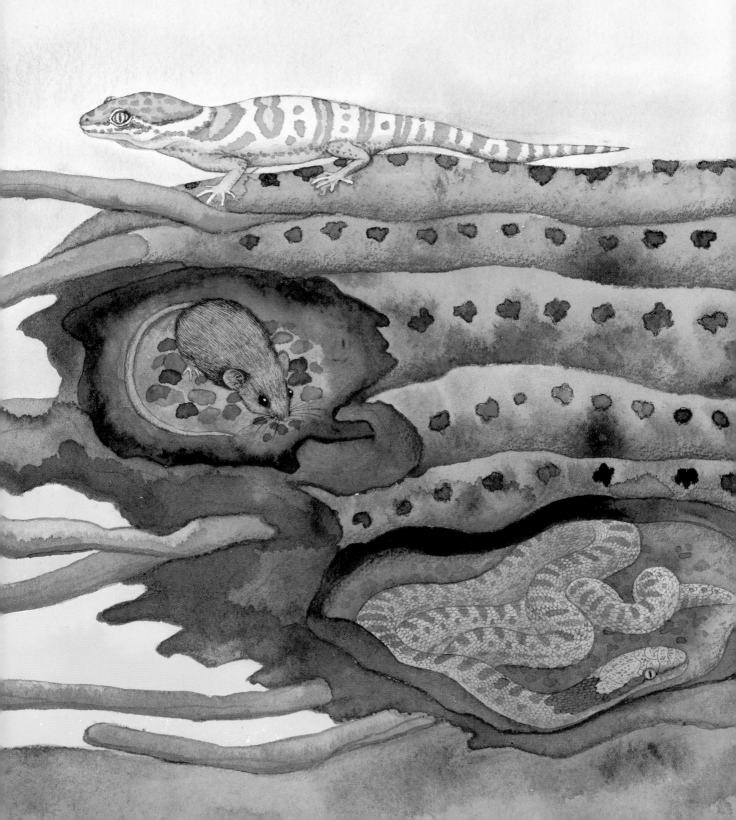

Deep inside, water is released as
the saguaro decomposes, and the
aquatic beetle swims through the
channels. A large hister beetle
probes the dark tunnels in search
of fly larvae and small insects.
The stripe-tailed scorpion looks for
prey amidst the rubble, while a
giant millipede searches for
decaying saguaro tissue to feed on.

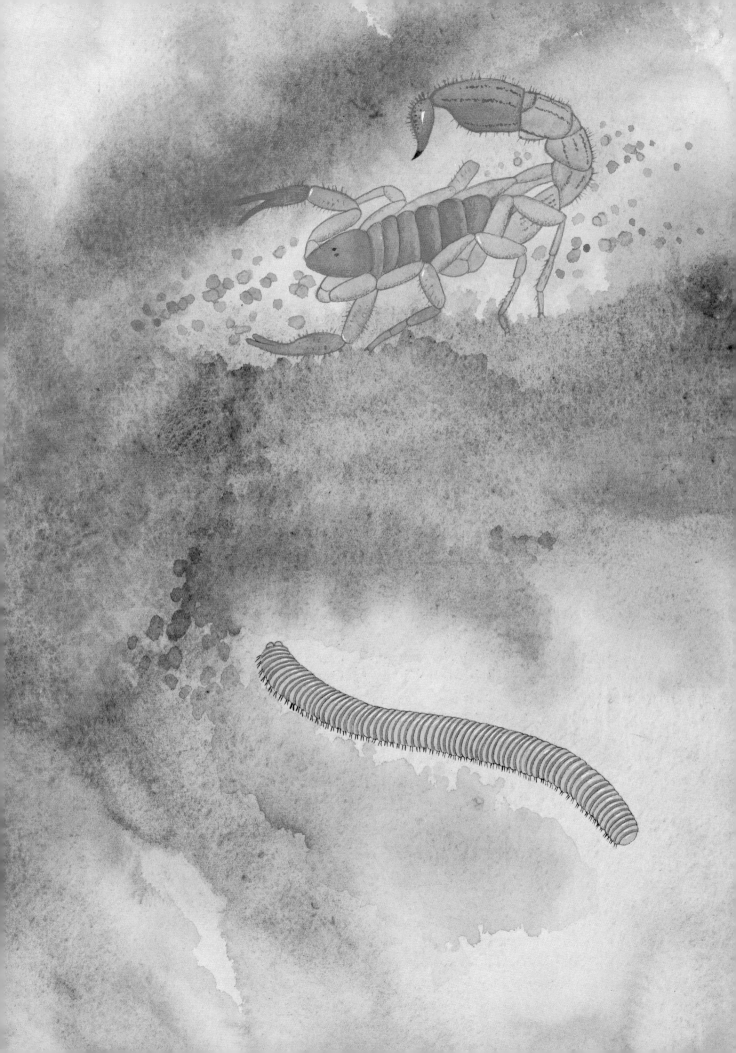

While one saguaro dies, another begins its new life. Each fruit-bearing saguaro produces millions of seeds, but most are eaten before they can sprout. The seeds that do germinate grow so slowly that the tiny saguaros are easily knocked over by animals or washed away by flash floods.

The only saguaros that have a chance of survival are those that begin their growth in the shelter of a "nurse plant." The canopy of the larger tree protects the young saguaro, and for many years it grows safely. Eventually the nurse plant dies, but by then the saguaro is strong enough to stand alone. After fifty years, it begins to produce flowers and fruit. After seventy-five years, the saguaro's arms start to appear. . . .

Saguaro seeds   Four-month-old seedlings   Two years old

Twelve years old

When it is one hundred fifty years old,
the cactus giant towers quietly
over the desert.